Microcomputers
in the
Classroom

By Justine C. Baker

Library of Congress Catalog Card Number 82-060799
ISBN 0-87367-179-1
Copyright © 1982 by the Phi Delta Kappa Educational Foundation
Bloomington, Indiana

This fastback is sponsored by the five chapters of Phi Delta Kappa in Area 7Q, which made a generous contribution toward publication costs. The chapters are:

Clearwater-St. Petersburg Florida
Bradenton-Sarasota Florida
Tampa Florida
Southwest Florida
Collier County Florida

Table of Contents

Introduction

During a recent Christmas season a popular television commercial showed a typical American family seated in front of the television set in their home. This family was not viewing its favorite situation comedy, TV movie, or local sporting event; rather it was enjoying the animated graphics, titillating sounds, and challenging interaction of a home video game. The sponsor of the commercial, Atari Incorporated, is one of several companies selling video games that are connected to a home television set, which serves as a video monitor.

The photo below shows a family playing Atari's version of the popular video arcade game PAC-MAN. The children are using joysticks to guide PAC-MAN through a maze. PAC-MAN is a yellow circle with an eye and a mouth. Points are scored when the hero voraciously consumes dots that appear on the screen. But while he is busy gobbling up dots, enemy ghosts challenge PAC-MAN. This menacing group must be eaten by PAC-MAN; otherwise, they will eat him.

Family enjoying PAC-MAN, a computer video game.

Excitement mounts as the children try to react quickly enough to place PAC-MAN in the right places at the right times in order to overcome his pursuing enemies.

Across America children and adults of all ages are enjoying video computer games. Some games can be played with equipment similar to that shown in the photo. More sophisticated games are played with larger, more complex microcomputer systems. Still other games can be played with microprocessor toys. In video arcades, games are played on pinball-type machines; and these amazing electronic games seem to be everywhere—in casinos, in restaurants, in supermarkets, in academic institutions, in game shops, and even in private homes.

In addition to the ready availability of computer games, personal computers with a wide variety of programs can be purchased in local shopping centers. Hardly a day goes by that newspapers and magazines don't carry ads from such personal computer vendors as IBM, Apple,

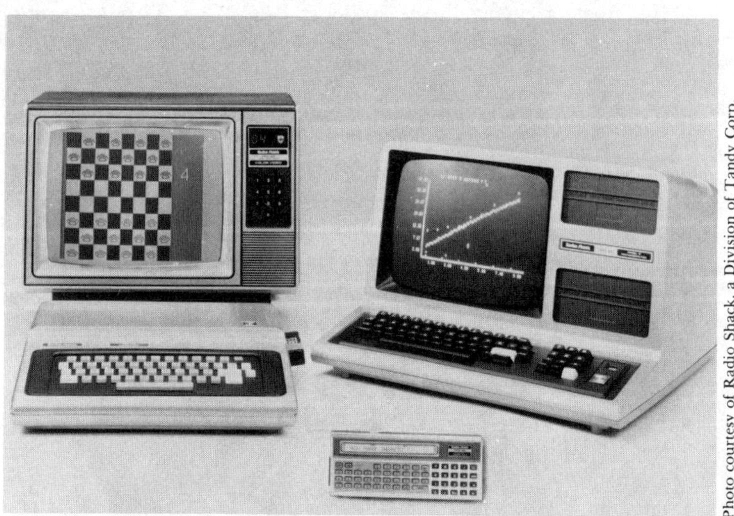

Three members of the TRS-80 line of microcomputers. From left to right: TRS-80 Color Computer with optional color monitor and Program Pak™ software, TRS-80 PC-1 Pocket Computer, and Model III Desk Top Microcomputer. The pocket computer, containing two 4-bit CMOS microprocessors, weighs only 6 ounces!

Atari, Radio Shack, Commodore, Heath, and Texas Instruments, all of whom are flooding the marketplace with newer, better, or cheaper models. A University of Southern California study projects that by the end of the decade half of the homes in the United States will have a personal computer system that can act as cooking consultant, financial planner, teacher, and plaything (Capron and Williams, 1982).

With the proliferation of computer games for children and personal computers for the home, the question naturally arises, What about microcomputers in the schools? What is the potential of this amazing technology for instruction?

Computer hardware vendors are bombarding the schools with tempting offers to "revolutionize your teaching." At conferences and workshops across the country, educators are learning much about the use of microcomputers in the classroom. Teachers, administrators, and parents are all seeking information about microcomputers and their application to instruction.

This fastback has two primary purposes: to provide in a brief format relevant facts about microcomputers and to encourage educators to take the initiative in making effective use of this new technology in their schools.

I begin by discussing the components of computer literacy and describing what microcomputers are and how they work. This is followed by a summary of recent surveys on the use of microcomputers in the schools and a review of research on microprocessor toys and video computer games. The section on teacher education explores what colleges and universities are doing to prepare teachers in the instructional uses of computers. The next section on organizational support focuses on what computer manufacturers, software vendors, professional organizations, an oil company, and the federal government are doing to help "computerize" the curriculum. The fastback concludes with a brief futures scenario on microcomputers in education. It could be quite an exciting future!

What Is Computer Literacy?

Computer literacy is a term that came into use in the late 1960s. Originally computer literacy meant learning about computers through reading and study. Little or nothing in the way of personal contact with computers was encompassed in the meaning of computer literacy. However, the work of such pioneers as Patrick Suppes of Stanford University and Seymour Papert of M.I.T. showed how computers could be used successfully as tools for instruction by students at all grade levels. Throughout the 1970s other computer educators began to provide students with hands-on experience with computers. The net result of such fruitful endeavors is that today the term *computer literacy* has broadened its scope to include *knowledge of* and *experience with* computers. Under this broadened scope computer literacy includes experience with computer-assisted instruction (CAI) involving drill, tutorial, or simulation lessons. Problem solving by computer also falls within the scope of the term; that is, students write their own programs or use available programs to solve problems in different school subjects. Because computer games and simulations have become so popular, entertainment via this medium could also be included in computer literacy. Lastly, the term includes an awareness of the potential that computer technology has for the future—for jobs and for everyday living.

From the foregoing discussion, it is easy to see that computer literacy could be woven into the curriculum at every level from kindergarten through graduate school. For educators, perhaps the place to begin to develop computer literacy is by learning what microcomputers are and how they work. This is the focus of the next chapter.

Microcomputers—Defined and Explained

Hidden beneath the plastic exteriors of all the electronic games, such as those mentioned in the introduction, is a remarkable element called a microprocessor. Microprocessors are found in microwave ovens, handheld calculators, late-model cameras, industrial robots, household appliances, gasoline pumps, and new automobiles as well as in games and toys. The versatility of the microprocessor is its ability to "think" and act in accordance with a set of instructions that constitutes a program. In short, a microprocessor is what its name suggests—a tiny processor of information.

A microcomputer is a small computer with a microprocessor brain

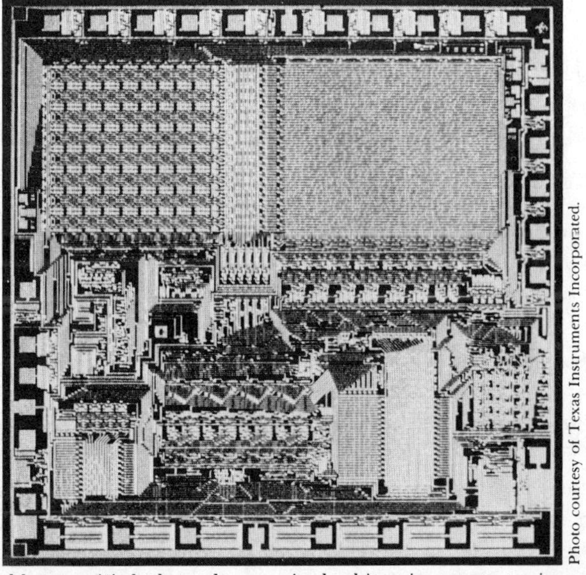

This highly magnified photo shows a single-chip microcomputer invented at Texas Instruments in 1971. This member of the TMS1000 family of 4-bit, single-chip microcomputers is used in such products as microwave ovens, electronic games, television tuners, dishwashers, sewing machines, and gasoline pumps.

that serves as a central processing unit. The term *central processing unit* needs clarification. To process information one must be able to see and interpret; that is, to read the symbols that make up a language. The computer, whatever its size, does precisely this. The process might be compared to building a model airplane from a kit of parts. To do this, an individual must read the instructions and then assemble the parts. The human brain coordinates the eyes and hands to work together to complete the model. In a similar fashion, a microcomputer can read its program (instruction manual) and run off, for example, a list of students' grade-point averages. The microcomputer's central processing unit, or its microprocessor, "instructs" the electronic components to do the calculations to complete the job.

Engineers have designed digital computers to distinguish between two states—*off* and *on*. Depending on the type of computer hardware, these states are controlled by 1) the absence of an electrical current versus the presence of a current, 2) low voltage versus high voltage, 3) the absence of a magnetized spot versus the presence of a magnetized spot, 4) counterclockwise magnetic core orientation versus clockwise magnetic core orientation, and 5) the absence of a magnetic bubble versus the presence of a magnetic bubble. The off/on coding scheme uses a base two number system: We associate the "off" state with 0 and the "on" state with 1. Together these two symbols make up the computer's alphabet. Each symbol is called a *bit*, which is a shortened form of *bi*nary dig*it*.

Bits by themselves, however, are insufficient to convey an entire language that includes an alphabet, numerals, mathematical symbols, and punctuation marks. For this reason several bits are grouped together as units, each of which is called a *byte*. Usually eight adjacent bits form a byte. Each byte represents one character of information, such as a letter of the alphabet. Several different coding schemes are based on the byte. In one such scheme, the eight-unit bytes might represent 11000001 for A, 11000010 for B, 11101001 for Z, 11110000 for 0, 11111001 for 9, 01000000 for a blank, and 01011011 for $. More extensive to complete lists of such codes can be found in many computer textbooks.

In computer terminology, bytes are associated with storage, of which there are two kinds—primary and secondary. Storage refers to the amount of information a computer can hold. In the microcomputer, primary storage is known as random access memory (RAM).

Since a byte represents only one alphabetic or numerical character, it obviously takes many bytes to communicate the instructions for a computer program. For this reason, the prefixes "kilo" and "mega" are commonly found in computer literature. In computer terminology, K means kilobyte, 1024 (2^{10}) bytes, or roughly 1,000 bytes. A megabyte (M) is equivalent to 1024K (K^2) bytes, or 1,048,576 bytes. One megabyte, then, is approximately one million bytes.

In general, the size of a computer determines its primary storage capacity. Large computers, sometimes called mainframes, hold from one to 16 megabytes and sometimes more. Minicomputers, which are smaller than large computers but larger than microcomputers, usually hold between 64K bytes and 1 megabyte. Many microcomputers hold from 4K bytes to 64K bytes, and sometimes more, in primary storage. Microcomputer games usually need at least 16K bytes of random access memory.

The upper limits of microcomputer memory capacity are constantly being extended. For example, IBM's personal computers, first introduced in the summer of 1981, feature up to 256K bytes of main storage, with a minimum of 16K bytes. Radio Shack's TRS-80 Model 16, released during the second quarter of 1982, has 128K bytes of internal RAM and could be expanded to 512K bytes.

Closely related to computer size is its processing speed. For example, small computers can process an instruction involving addition of two numbers in less than a millisecond, or one-thousandth of a second. Large computers can process that same instruction in less than a microsecond, which is one-millionth of a second. Supercomputers can do better. Computers like the Cray-1 can process that instruction in less than a nanosecond, which is one-billionth of a second.

Another factor in classifying computers by size and processing speed is their word storage capacity. A "word," in computer technology is a collection of adjacent bits that comprise a common unit of information. Word lengths vary according to computer classification. Microcomputers have been associated with 8-bit words; minicomputers with 16-bit words; large computers, with 32-bit, 36-bit, or 48-bit words; supercomputers, with 64-bit words. Some newer model microcomputers now have the capacity for 16-bit words, which provides greater versatility and faster processing.

The connection between memory word length and computer processing speed is complex. Several variables are involved such as computer architecture (hardware design) and method of addressing (retrieval of instructions from storage). An analogy with speed reading might prove helpful here. Suppose two individuals, one of whom is a speed reader, decide to build that model airplane mentioned previously. The speed reader has the skill to see and interpret more words on each page of the instruction manual than does the other person who reads more slowly. Assume they have equal dexterity and that they start at the same time. The speed reader would build the plane first. Likewise, a microprocessor that reads longer words in a certain time period

The Radio Shack TRS-80 Model 16 Computer, which features 16-bit technology, dual processor architecture, and a multi-user operating system, is the company's fastest and most powerful model.

would orchestrate its microcomputer to complete the assigned task faster than a similar microcomputer whose microprocessor reads shorter words in that same time period.

With the above fundamentals in mind, let's now take a closer look at how a microcomputer functions. A microcomputer is composed of four interconnected parts: 1) a central processing unit (CPU), 2) a storage unit, 3) an input device, and 4) an output device. The CPU is composed of three parts: 1) a control unit, 2) an arithmetic/logic unit (ALU), and 3) additional storage locations known as registers, which are not part of primary storage.

Just as the conductor of an orchestra reads the score line by line and directs musicians to play the music, the control unit reads the instructions entered from the input device and directs the ALU, the registers, and the output device to process the instructions (memory words). For example, the ALU does the adding, subtracting, multiplying, dividing, and other mathematical functions. The registers act as conduits for data flowing back and forth between the CPU and main memory. The input and output devices serve as the link between the user and the CPU. The input device carries instructions from the user to main memory. The output device carries information from main memory back to the user.

The heart and brain of a microcomputer is a microprocessor chip. The chip is a tiny, thin slice of semiconductor material made of chemically treated silicon. Although sizes vary, a typical chip is about 6mm square by ¼mm thick, small enough to fit on a person's fingernail! It seems incredible that so small a piece of crystal can control and direct the host of functions that computers perform. The chip contains thousands of microscopic switching circuits, known as gates, that conduct electricity and process information.

Modern microcomputers feature one or more microprocessors and a set of memory chips that are connected to one or more circuit boards, called cards. The input and output devices are connected to the electronic ensemble inside the computer cabinet. The most common input device is the familiar typewriter-like keyboard. Two types of soft-copy (screen) output devices are widely used. The first is a video monitor, which displays the data from the main memory. The computers used in

The Texas Instruments TMS99000 is the industry's first third-generation 16-bit microprocessor family. This highly magnified photo shows a chip for advanced microprocessors, a controller CPU. It performs a specific set of controlled functions such as input/output processing.

many business offices are examples of this type. The second is a standard television set, fitted with an RF modulator, which is used as the output unit for home video games. Both kinds of output devices can also display input, for example, when a user submits a self-written program.

The types of microcomputers described above have a serious drawback, because they have no capacity for permanent storage of programs. This means that when the power is turned off the programs are lost. To rectify this, secondary storage, also known as auxiliary storage, is needed. Today many microcomputers provide for this secondary storage by having permanent programs on floppy disks, also known as diskettes. These disks, 5¼ inches or 8 inches in diameter, resemble 45 rpm phonograph records. Information can be added to (written) or retrieved from (read) the diskette by way of the disk drive mechanism that is connected to the other modules in the microcomputer.

Many microcomputers are now designed to support a variety of extensions beyond the basic microcomputer system just described. The Apple II Plus microcomputer system, for example, uses **BASIC** as its "native" computer language. But another language called Pascal can also be used simply by purchasing an additional electronics card, containing at least 16K bytes of extra memory and a Pascal compiler on a diskette. Or COBOL can be added to that same system by adding a Zilog Z80 card needed to execute programs in that language.

Other possibilities exist. An electronics card that allows a microcomputer to converse with a larger computer at another site can be added. This requires a modulator-demodulator unit called a modem that is connected to the microcomputer and the user's phone. The boxlike modem converts digital pulses from the microcomputer to analog waveforms suitable for transmission over telephone lines. Retranslation is needed at the receiving end via a modem linked to the host computer system. Then, after the information is processed by the larger computer, the modulation-demodulation cycle is repeated. Among other accessories are hard-copy (paper dispensing) printers.

Because the latest-model microcomputers have the flexibility to accept numerous attachments that extend the capabilities of the existing system, they are very attractive for home and school uses. Also, the extra accessories can be purchased over a period of time, which makes budgeting for them more feasible.

A Brief History of Microcomputers

Some acquaintance with the history of microcomputers is certainly a part of computer literacy. What is remarkable is how far we have come in the short period of time since 1969.

In 1969 a team of scientists at Intel of California, under the direction of Ted Hoff, succeeded in building an arithmetic/logic unit on a single integrated circuit chip. The Intel electronic engineers had achieved a breakthrough. By 1971 the Hoff team had created a central processing unit on a chip. The first microprocessor, called the Intel 4004, consisted of 2,250 transistors in an area smaller than 1/6 by 1/8 inches. Yet, in computational power, this tiny chip of negligible thickness was almost equal to the mammoth ENIAC, an acronym for Electronic Numerical Integrator and Computer, the first all-electronic, large-scale, general-purpose computer, which became operational in 1945. For purposes of comparison, consider that the ENIAC contained 18,000 vacuum tubes;

was 100 feet long, 10 feet wide, and 3 feet deep; and weighed 30 tons. It could perform a multiplication in about 3 milliseconds. Computer technology has come a long way since ENIAC!

By 1972 Intel had created another microprocessor known as the 8008, an improvement over the 4004. Whereas the 4004 understood and processed a 4-bit instruction set, the more powerful 8008 understood and processed an 8-bit instruction set. The Intel 8008 ushered in the hobby computer generation, the first of three distinguishable stages in microcomputer systems.

The years 1972 to 1976 marked the hobby computer stage. During those years engineering-minded individuals assembled their own microcomputers from parts sold in kits. One of the most popular of these kits, which sold for about $500, was the MITS Altair 8800. This kit featured the Intel 8080, which was invented in 1973 as an improved version of the 8008. During that period other companies were competing with Intel for their share of the ever-growing microprocessor market. Among them were Texas Instruments, Fairchild, Rockwell, National Semiconductor, Motorola, and Zilog. Also during this period, Steven Jobs and Stephen Wozniak, both hobby computer builders, formed a microcomputer company that was to be known as Apple Computer.

Commodore Business Machines was the first company to announce fully-assembled personal computers in 1976. Commodore's Personal Electronic Transactor (PET) micros were ready for marketing in October 1977. In 1977 Apple Computer was producing its personal computers. Joining these two companies was the Tandy Corporation, maker of the Radio Shack TRS-80 line of personal computers. The second generation of microcomputer systems had begun—the era of the personal computer.

The third generation of microcomputer systems is known as the workstation. Initiated around 1981, the workstation stage overlaps the personal computer stage. Workstations are microcomputers whose advanced hardware and operating systems permit more extensive memory access and considerably greater speed than the typical personal computer. The distinctive feature of a workstation is its resource sharing capability. For example, if a personal computer is elec-

TRS-80 Videotex™ Two-Way Information Retrieval System that allows a user to communicate with national information networks like Dow Jones and CompuServe. The user must connect a telephone to the microcomputer, which features a built-in modem to convey digital information via telephone lines. The user can get such information as stock market reports and daily news events.

tronically linked to other personal computers in a local area network or to a large computer in a telecommunications network, then that personal computer is a workstation. Those who might use such a facility are office workers, researchers, product developers, and even students. The workstation makes possible data base access and retrieval and extensive program writing and reading. In time, it is quite possible that most personal computers will evolve into workstations. Given the progress in microcomputer technology in just a decade, it is mind-boggling to consider what the next decade will hold.

Use of Microcomputers in Education

What is the extent of microcomputer use in the schools? How are they being used? What evaluation has been done? Do students learn from video games? These are the questions addressed in this chapter. With the rapid changes in the microcomputer field, the answers have to be tentative. But one thing is certain; a lot is happening. What is reported here may soon be out of date, but it provides basic information for those who are considering the use of microcomputers in their schools.

Extent of Use

A survey, conducted in October 1980 and released in March 1981 under the auspices of the National Center for Education Statistics (NCES), provides the following information on computer use in the schools. Of the 15,834 U.S. school districts, 48% provided students with access to at least one microcomputer or computer terminal. (A computer terminal is an input/output device electronically connected to a computer larger than a micro.) More than twice as many districts provided microcomputers rather than terminals. A more precise statistic is that approximately 22,000 public school buildings had at least one microcomputer or computer terminal available to students for instructional use. These schools represented 50% of all secondary schools and 14% of all elementary schools. Among school districts there was a combined total of almost 52,000 microcomputers and terminals available to students for instructional purposes.

The survey found that approximately 18% of those districts that did not offer instructional computing services planned to implement such usage within three years. Most of these were small districts with student populations under 2,500. Many of the other districts without computers were indecisive about future plans to use computers in the curriculum.

In terms of how computers were used, the survey found that developing computer literacy was the most frequently mentioned goal. Other frequently mentioned uses were learning enrichment in specific subject areas and challenge for high achievers. Remedial and compensatory applications were listed by fewer than half the responding districts.

Over 40% of the respondents called for teacher training and a greater range of instructional computer programs and materials. Other needs cited by about one-third of the responding districts were: 1) assistance in planning instructional computer programs, 2) technical assistance services in support of program operations, and 3) financial assistance.

Another survey, conducted by Market Data Retrieval, a market research firm in Westport, Connecticut, dealt with microcomputer use only. During July to September 1981 this firm telephoned representatives of 15,442 school districts, which include 84,226 public school buildings. Its report, published in October 1981, provides lots of data and identifies trends concerning use of microcomputers.

This survey found that among small school districts (under 1,200 students) fewer than one of three had microcomputer facilities; in larger school districts (over 5,000 students) two of three had microcomputer facilities. Furthermore, this survey found nearly 16,000 buildings of the total number surveyed had at least one microcomputer. The number of districts with microcomputers was 6,441. By school type, the survey reported 5,884 of 53,268 elementary schools had microcomputers; 2,585 of 10,106 junior high schools had microcomputers; 6,051 of 15,589 senior high schools had microcomputers; and 798 of 5,262 special and combined schools had microcomputers. The survey identified 33,281 schools that do not currently have microcomputers, but that are in user districts, as "prime prospects" to purchase personal computers.

The data on microcomputer sales from the MDR survey showed that in 1980 home sales amounted to $120 million; school sales amounted to $35 million. Estimates for sales by 1985 were $475 million for home, $145 million for school. These kinds of data indicate that computer use in the schools is already widespread and will continue to grow rapidly in the years ahead.

Data about microcomputer use in higher education can be found in a study by Aycock, Frankowski, and Franta. Based on a survey conducted in 1981, these researchers found that 54% of the 103 survey respondents reported that their schools had their first microcomputer by the end of 1978. Although homebrew systems had been acquired by some postsecondary schools prior to 1977, that year represented the turning point for acquisition of micros. The commercial availability of Apple, Commodore, and Radio Shack personal computers in 1977 sparked the beginning of large-scale acquisition of microcomputers on the college campus. Nonetheless, 14 respondents indicated that their school had no microcomputers.

An interesting finding from this survey was that mainly individual professors—not the institutional computer centers—first brought microcomputers onto the university campus. Homebrew systems gave professors a measure of personal control. They could do such things as monitor their own laboratory experiments without the involvement of computer center personnel, and they didn't have to wait for the computer center to install this new technology.

The survey found the following uses of computers in the higher education institutions that responded: entry level programming courses, 44%; advanced programming courses, 30%; micro design courses, 35%; CAI, 42%; general research programming, 39%; text preparation, 38%; monitoring laboratory experiments, 49%; laboratory record keeping, 31%; data processing, 33%; student records, 11%; microcomputer research, 34%; and other, 15%.

Evaluation of Microcomputer Courseware

In 1981 Educational Products Information Exchange (EPIE) Institute of Stony Brook, New York, released its first of many projected computer courseware surveys. Working in conjunction with the Microcomputer Resource Center at Teachers College Columbia University, EPIE evaluated six large commercial courseware packages.

Complete results are reported in the EPIE publication, *Microcomputer Courseware/Microprocessor Games* (1981).

All the courseware packages evaluated used floppy disks or cassette tapes or both. The audiences for these courses, for the most part, were elementary, junior high, or older students lacking basic skills in mathematics or reading. EPIE evaluated each course on a long list of features including: readability of textual displays; integration of graphics, if any, within textual frames; use of cues and prompts; ease of using the programs; record-management capabilities; and feedback for correct and incorrect answers. The evaluation also considered branching formats for new and review material and even printed materials, such as teachers' manuals.

General findings follow. The EPIE report noted that there is a greater need for software that can teach critical thinking, problem solving, and higher-order skills, such as application, analysis, synthesis, and evaluation. EPIE also recommended that more microcomputer software should be directed toward older students. Evaluators felt that too many programs had already been developed for elementary arithmetic drill and practice lessons, probably because these lessons are relatively easy to construct. They expressed caution about the microcomputer becoming stereotyped as a drill and practice tool, when it can do so much more; for example, manage instruction by keeping records of student progress. EPIE suggested large courseware packages incorporate such capabilities. The study encouraged publishers to develop a range of courseware so that the microcomputer could serve the total school curriculum.

Evaluation and Research on Video Computer Games

Since microcomputer applications in the form of video games are so popular with students of all ages, the question arises, Should video games be used in the curriculum? What are children learning with these fascinating games? EPIE, in the second half of its study of microcomputer courseware, conducted some interesting evaluation research, which provides some answers but raises other questions for educators.

EPIE selected eight microprocessor games for evaluation with disadvantaged students in kindergarten through grade seven in four New

York area schools. The eight games used were: "Dataman," "Math Master," "Lil Genius," "Little Professor," "Quiz Kid," "Speak and Spell," "Spelling B," and "Quiz Wiz." The first five deal with mathematics, the other three with spelling and facts. The games had been selected originally because of their popularity.

Since none of the subjects had ever used any of the games prior to the study, it was possible to use pre- and posttests to determine whether learning in mathematics or spelling or both had taken place. EPIE researchers found inconclusive evidence of new learning taking place insofar as use of the games was concerned. They stressed that students who had used the games showed no significant gain either in mathematics or spelling proficiency. Furthermore, they said that these microprocessor games do not teach what is not already known; therefore their instructional value is questionable. The evaluators found that, at best, the games review, and thereby reinforce, arithmetic operations and spelling strategies at about the fourth- or fifth-grade levels.

Although the children enjoyed playing with these small handheld electronic gadgets, observers noted that at times some youngsters were both bored and frustrated. Overall, the favorites were two games manufactured by Texas Instruments, "Dataman" and "Speak and Spell." Both games provide superior reinforcement and display capacities. The first game lists at $22; the second game, containing a sophisticated voice circuit, lists at $55. Given these prices in comparison to those of traditional textbooks, teachers participating in this study agreed these games should not replace printed materials. Moreover, the teachers' consensus was that for the microprocessor games to be of motivational value, at least one game should be available for each pair of children.

In summary, the EPIE study concluded that microprocessor games have limited instructional value, other than reinforcement. Their major limiting factor apparently is their size. For example, display panels on the math games are generally confined to small, usually rectangular, areas at the top of these little calculator-like devices. Researchers noticed that some children who could correctly answer arithmetic problems that were presented in vertical format on paper were unable to answer the same problems when they were presented in horizontal format on the games. Additionally, researchers noticed another kind of display panel problem with the spelling games lacking audio capability. Line drawings in the display panel provided clues concerning nouns to be spelled at the miniature keyboards, but because of the ambiguous nature of several of these drawings, some children misinterpreted the intended noun and spelled another word instead. Even when the children spelled their word correctly, the game would tell them it was incorrect. Thus at times, some microprocessor games exert a kind of negative instructional influence.

The EPIE evaluation of video games deserves the attention of educators; but since these games are relatively new, much more research is needed. The research of Thomas W. Malone is a promising beginning toward the scientific study of computer-supported learning activities. His Ph.D. dissertation at Stanford University focuses on what features make computer games so intrinsically motivating. In a paper, based on his dissertation, "What Makes Things Fun to Learn? A Study of Intrinsically Motivating Computer Games," he examines two questions.

1. Why are computer games so captivating?
2. How can the features that make computer games captivating be used to make learning—especially learning with computers—interesting and enjoyable?

Malone's answers to these questions, although incomplete, provide empirical groundwork for designing a chip-age curriculum.

Using a variety of video games and modified versions of these games with both young and older students, he found that challenge (having a goal and keeping a score), curiosity, and fantasy were the elements that contributed to the intrinsic motivation of the most popular games. These three elements are also the basis for all intellectual activity. Those involved in the design of instructional programs for microcomputers should pay heed to these findings.

A complete discussion of what can be learned from video computer games is beyond the scope of this fastback, but a few games deserve a brief examination.

PAC-MAN, generally considered a motor-skills game, comes in different versions. The arcade version is perhaps the most challenging and complex.

Ken Uston, author of *Mastering PAC-MAN*, states, "The characteristic that attracted me to PAC-MAN is that a predetermined plan is far more important for a high score than is a high degree of physical coordination." He goes on to explain seven basic patterns a player can use to get a high score. According to Uston, a player who memorizes, practices, and perfectly executes four or five patterns in his book should be able to qualify for "PAC-Master" classification.

It could be argued that pattern recognition is one of the six basic process abilities in elementary mathematics; that is, the ability to recognize regular patterns is an important skill in mastering mathematics. Transfer of this kind of skill from PAC-MAN to school mathematics is plausible.

There are other learning considerations in regard to PAC-MAN and other video computer games that fall under the rubric of spatial ability. There is substantial consensus among researchers that spatial ability is composed of at least two factors: spatial visualization and spatial orientation. Mark G. McGee defines the two terms as follows:

> Spatial visualization involves the ability to mentally rotate, manipulate, and twist two- and three-dimensional stimulus objects. Spatial orientation involves the comprehension of the arrangement of elements within a visual stimulus pattern, the aptitude to remain unconfused by the changing orientation in which a spatial configuration may be presented, and the ability to determine spatial orientation with respect to one's body.

Given the preceding definitions, it can be inferred that spatial orientation is a factor in how well the player does in the game. In other words, a person's spatial orientation aptitude could contribute to high PAC-MAN scores. A corollary question that needs to be researched is, Does playing such video games as PAC-MAN actually improve one's spatial orientation aptitude?

In an article, "Video Jocks Versus the Quarter-Eaters," Jack Lule cited the remarkable achievement of a Philadelphia teenager, Derek Simons, who scored 18 million points during a 38-hour marathon playing the game called "Asteroids." "Asteroids" is a space game in which a player operates a triangular spaceship and attempts to manuever his spacecraft to safety while dodging dangerous asteroid rocks and deadly flying saucers.

Derek Simons said he employs mathematical and logical concepts to win spectacularly at "Asteroids." In addition, he, like Uston, maps out mental strategies in advance of his actual physical moves. In effect, he is using aptitude in mathematics and logic to achieve high scores in "Asteroids." The question germane to education is, Will youngsters who avidly play video computer games over extended time periods do better in school subjects requiring spatial, mathematical, and logical aptitudes such as geometry, computer programming, and chemistry?

My own position is that the answer to this question is related to the chronological age of the player. For example, children 8 to 14 years of age who continue to play microcomputer games over a period of years could derive an "achievement effect" from their extensive game playing. Hence, it is possible such youngsters would do better than their non-game playing school counterparts. Also, since there is substantial evidence that males have consistently shown superiority over females in spatial ability tasks, it is possible that girls could improve their spatial skills by playing games like PAC-MAN when they are young. Standard spatial ability tests have shown the gender difference to emerge after the age of 11 or 12; hence, video computer game playing might prove quite beneficial for young girls between the ages of 8 to 11. This is a hypothesis crying out for corroborative support from experimental evidence.

Let us now consider a game that is more directly educational. A stellar example is Atari's "SCRAM," an acronym for *Start Cutting Right Away, Man.* That phrase can be traced back to a group of scientists, under the leadership of Enrico Fermi at the University of Chicago, who started up the world's first nuclear reactor in December 1942. The phrase refers to the process for halting the reactor, which, once started, could be stopped only by cutting a rope attached to a control rod suspended directly over the reactor.

Insofar as skills are concerned, Atari claims that "SCRAM" develops the player's ability to: 1) think logically and objectively; 2) see patterns in complex systems; 3) see cause-and-effect relationships; and

4) analyze problems and solve them effectively. "SCRAM," intended for 12-year-olds to adults, is more than a game; it is a kind of computer-assisted instruction, endowed with challenge, curiosity, and fantasy, the three elements Malone identifies as associated with intrinsic motivation.

Any science enthusiast or inquisitive youngster who purchases "SCRAM" is in for an educational treat. First the viewer witnesses the building of a nuclear power station; then comes the issuance of the plant operation license from the Nuclear Regulatory Commission. At the conclusion of these entertaining and instructional events, the simulation part of the game begins. The game tests the player's ability to use quickly and accurately the material previously learned from viewing and interacting with the simulation.

The simulation part of "SCRAM" instructs cleverly as the following illustration shows. Players must be able to decide whether a valve or a pump within one of several loops has been damaged. If players see a rise in hot leg temperature with a concomitant drop in cold leg temperature within a certain loop, then they conclude that a pump has failed. Given this information, the players must check further to see which kind of pump has failed. If the players notice that the steam level in the steam generator has dropped below normal, they infer that not enough water is entering the steam generator. Their final deduction is that a feedwater pump has failed. They must immediately send in workers to fix that particular pump.

This kind of if-then reasoning accompanied by correct decision making represents the highest level of problem solving. The concatenation of at least two rules to generate a new rule is called higher-order rule production, which is a form of critical thinking. To inculcate and elicit this kind of thinking from students is the reason most educators choose teaching as a career!

This brief discussion of the learning potential of video games serves only as a prelude to the research that is needed so that we make the appropriate use of microcomputer technology in our schools. Some have expressed concern over the time youngsters consume and the money they spend on video games (not unlike the complaints about comic books and television in years past). Others have criticized so-called "educational" video games as nothing more than high-priced drill and practice workbooks. These criticisms may be valid, but there is great potential for developing microcomputer hardware and courseware along sound pedagogical principles. It remains for educators to take the leadership in this endeavor.

Curriculum Considerations

In *The Computer in the School: Tutor, Tool, Tutee,* Robert Taylor of Teachers College Columbia University identifies three broad modes of computer usage in schools: as tutor, as tool, and as tutee. Although the book focuses on computers in general, the modes apply equally well to the microcomputer.

As a tutor, the computer teaches its user. An example is computer-assisted instruction (CAI). At its best, CAI can manage instruction as well, by keeping records of student progress and by prescribing lessons for subsequent study. In this mode the computer is intended to complement the classroom teacher, not replace that teacher.

This student is using the microcomputer for instruction. The disk drive unit is the small box situated to the right of the video monitor.

As a tool, the computer provides a variety of services: preparing payrolls, inventories, and budgets; playing games and music; managing administrative and library records; processing literary texts and artistic designs; administering and evaluating tests; calculating statistics of data sets and roots of mathematical equations; and simulating scientific experiments, space flights, and entrepreneurial ventures.

As a tutee, the computer is taught by a person how to function both as a tutor and a tool. For example, students can write programs to tell the computer how to be a tool. Program specialists can write programs to tell the computer how to act as a tutor. To teach a computer, in a language it understands (i.e., it can translate), how to solve a problem or how to prepare a lesson with concomitant sound and graphics requires critical and analytical thinking skills. These kinds of problem-solving skills exemplify the end product of good education.

A noteworthy example of how a school actually incorporates computers in the curriculum is provided by the Moreland School in the Shaker Heights School District in Ohio. Forty-one Radio Shack and Atari microcomputers are housed throughout the school: 18 are in the computer lab, three in the library, and 20 in classrooms. Classes are assigned to the computer lab on a regular basis so that students can use personal computers for individualized instruction. Teachers assign, or pupils select, a variety of computer software materials. In either case, the microcomputer complements traditional instruction by reinforcing or expanding skills and knowledge. In the more formal classroom environments, students use microcomputers for similar purposes.

In Moreland's comprehensive computer literacy program, students are allowed to work at their own pace by typing at the keyboards simple commands in BASIC (Beginner's All-purpose Symbolic Instruction Code). While advancing through the computer literacy curriculum, students learn about the history of computers, use of computers in various disciplines, influence of computers in society, identification of computer parts, and how the computer works. Eventually, students develop competencies in writing and correcting their own programs.

A number of adjunct activities further enrich Moreland's computer literacy program. Students can use micros in the library to develop special skills, such as vocabulary building and alphabetizing. Also, all students from grades one through six have the opportunity to learn typing so they can use the computer keyboard; first-graders have two 20-minute typing instruction periods a week. Other students are encouraged to continue the program on their own time at recess periods or after school. Optional activities include a computer club for youngsters in grades three through six and a computer games club for all children.

The Moreland model, with appropriate adaptations for specific school populations, could be implemented in other elementary, middle, and junior high schools. For secondary schools, the Association for Computing Machinery has recommended a one-year computer science course. This course, intended for all secondary schools, emphasizes the role of the computer as a multifaceted, problem-solving tool. Computer awareness topics, such as computer history, hardware and software functions, kinds of computer applications, and social and ethical implications are included. Programming assignments from the simple to the complex, in a language such as BASIC, are also part of the course. More details about this course appear in an article by Jean B. Rogers and Dick Austing (see references).

Some secondary schools have already implemented courses such as that described above. This general course serves as a foundation for subsequent courses. Once students have learned basic programming skills, they can transfer these skills to solving mensuration problems in trigonometry. Secretarial science students can use their background from the general course to undertake work on a word processor microcomputer.

There is currently considerable overlap in the general computer course from high school to the college level, so many freshmen and sophomores in college are taking courses similar to that described by Rogers and Austing. For college students, Pascal (named for Blaise Pascal, the 17th century French mathematician) rather than BASIC is preferred, since it is based on the principles of structured programming and is better suited to designing easy-to-read programs. However, depending on the academic background and vocational plans of the students, a computer awareness course coupled with data entry assignments, rather than formal programming, is a viable alternative.

One possible assignment is the entry of numeric data into a prewritten business program known as VisiCalc (short for "Visible Calculator").

Microcomputers can also be used in other ways in addition to the general college-level course. For example, students in business-oriented colleges use microcomputers to learn COBOL (*CO*mmon *B*usiness *O*riented *L*anguage) programming skills that they will later use in their jobs. Undergraduate and graduate students enrolled in large-scale, software engineering courses involving writing of lengthy programs are probably better served by minicomputers or large computers. However, the storage limitations of microcomputers can be overcome when they operate as workstations with access to larger computers. This is the next generation for microcomputers.

One cannot go into much depth when discussing curriculum considerations for microcomputers without confronting the issue of computer literacy for teachers. Much is happening in that area, as the next chapter will show.

Teacher Education in Computer Literacy

W hat do teachers have to know about computers in order to develop a computer literacy curriculum for students? James Poirot, Robert Taylor, and James Powell have identified seven universal competencies needed by *all* teachers. Paraphrased these competencies are: 1) ability to read, write, and execute simple programs; 2) ability to use educational application software; 3) ability to speak intelligently, although not necessarily as an expert, about computer terminology, especially in regard to hardware; 4) ability to recognize examples of the kinds of educational problems that can and cannot be solved by computers; 5) ability to locate and use alternate sources of up-to-date information on computing in education; 6) ability to discuss, at the level of an intelligent layperson, the history of computing in general and that of computing in education in particular; and 7) ability to discuss ethical or social issues regarding computing in general and of educational computing in particular. The authors believe these competencies, if integrated into existing teacher education programs, would prepare teachers at a minimal computer literacy level.

In 1976, when my fastback *Computers in the Curriculum* was published, a few universities were offering computer courses to practicing and prospective teachers. Teachers College Columbia University began offering an M.A. program in 1975 called "Computing and Education." However, at that time most instructional computing was conducted via time-sharing with mini and large computers. The appearance of fully assembled microcomputers in 1977 sparked an even greater need for teacher education in computing.

By 1979 the personal computer had made some inroads into the schools. With the microcomputer, teachers and students no longer were frustrated over waiting times to access a large computer, or waiting for the computer to respond to their commands once they were "on" the machine. Principals no longer had to worry about servicing and processing expenses. These kinds of headaches associated with time-sharing services had been removed, but other problems remained. Writing in the fall 1979 *AEDS Journal*, David Moursund cautioned the education community about some of these problems, citing shortages in hardware and software, lack of trained teachers, and lack of administrative support. However, universities and other organizations were already addressing these problems.

The March 1982 issue of *The Computing Teacher* carried a partial list of colleges and universities offering computer education courses for summer 1982. Spotlighted were 38 U.S. and eight Canadian institutions. Almost all schools listed microcomputers as part of their computer equipment; many also mentioned a variety of mini and large computers.

Most institutions listed more than one course offering. Microcomputer courses are commonly titled "Microcomputer Applications in the Classroom." Computer languages offered include LOGO, popular with elementary school students; BASIC, popular with high school students; PILOT, important for teachers who want to write their own courseware; and Pascal, now becoming popular with some high school students and already popular with many college students.

Degree offerings are mostly at the graduate level. In general, degrees in computer education for precollege teachers are granted upon successful completion of several computer education courses mixed with a number of courses in business, computer science, arts and sciences, or combinations thereof. Degrees for those individuals who either teach precollege teachers or collegiate computer science or business students are usually granted by departments and schools outside education. For example, the University of Pennsylvania currently offers a minimal number of computer courses to education majors at its Graduate School of Education, but education students can select many excellent high-powered courses at Penn's Moore School of Electrical Engineering, at the Wharton School, or in various academic departments of the university.

A partial list of those institutions offering degree programs in computers for precollege teachers include: Arizona State University, Teachers College Columbia University, Florida Atlantic University, Lehigh University, Lesley College Graduate School, Nova University, Ontario Institute for Studies in Education, Pace University, Pennsylvania State University, Southern Illinois University, Southwest Texas

State University, Stanford University, SUNY at Albany, SUNY at Stony Brook, University of Calgary, University of Cincinnati, University of Delaware, University of Houston, University of Illinois, University of Kansas, University of Kentucky, University of Oklahoma, University of Oregon, University of Maine at Orono, and University of Tulsa.

New York University is considering a certificate program in Microcomputer Applications. University of British Columbia is awaiting approval for the M.Ed. in Computer Applications in Education and for an interdepartmental Ed.D. in Computer Applications in Education. University of Florida expects to establish, by September 1982, a Ph.D. program in curriculum and instruction that will be a joint offering between the School of Education and the Department of Computer Science in the College of Engineering. Barry University in Florida will have a computer program for teachers that will be given by the department of computer science.

Degree programs are not the only avenue for teachers' preparation in computer education. Many institutions are sponsoring workshops and conferences for teachers and administrators and publishing computer education materials. For example, Arizona State University has sponsored two national conferences on microcomputers and published the proceedings. Lesley College Graduate School in Cambridge, Massachusetts, sponsors an annual computer conference that features hands-on sessions and a series of lectures. Supported by a grant from the EXXON Education Foundation, the University of Illinois has published *The Illinois Series on Educational Application of Computers*. The M.I.T. Artificial Intelligence Laboratory also disseminates publications about computers. Several of these booklets contain information about Seymour Papert's outstanding work with elementary school youngsters.

Besides universities, support for teacher computer education is available from many organizations, including the federal government. Space permits only a few of these to be mentioned in the next section. Their addresses are found in the Appendix.

Organizational Support for Instructional Use of Microcomputers

Apple Computer Inc., through its Foundation for the Advancement of Computer Aided Education, seeks to improve learning in the schools by providing to qualified organizations and individuals hardware equipment for innovative computer-based projects. Steven Jobs, Apple's chairman of the board, has persuaded legislators to introduce bills to Congress to allow substantial tax deductions to manufacturers who donate microcomputers to public and private elementary and secondary schools. Voting on bills HR 5573 and S 2281 is expected to take place before the end of 1982.

Atari, a Warner Communications Company, sponsors a most interesting software development competition. Although not directly aimed at the schools, products emanating from the Atari Software Acquisition Program Contest could benefit students. Besides offering annual cash prizes to those who write top-of-the-line programs for Atari 400 and 800 computers, the company also awards computer products or cash stipends through its Institute for Educational Action Research.

Radio Shack, a division of Tandy Corporation, is interested in promoting the development of education courseware. Toward this goal, that company has pledged $500,000 in equipment.

The Association for Computing Machinery (ACM) has played a leadership role in "computerizing" education at all levels. ACM spokespersons have consulted with schools and colleges on computer literacy; and ACM publications, rich with computer-based learning ideas, have helped educators to initiate and improve computer education programs.

CONDUIT, a research and development clearinghouse for computer-based couseware, is located at the University of Iowa. With a professional staff interested in design, development, packaging, and evaluation, it provides high quality curriculum materials on computer-assisted instruction—particularly at the postsecondary level. CONDUIT services include: 1) disseminating general information about computer usage in higher education; 2) providing specific information to authors and developers of computer-based materials; and 3) issuing reports on CONDUIT-reviewed and -tested materials. This organization publishes a quarterly journal called *PIPELINE* that deals with computers and their instructional uses.

MicroSIFT, an acronym for Microcomputer Software and Information for Teachers, is a project of the Northwest Regional Educational Laboratory in Portland, Oregon. It serves as a clearinghouse for microcomputer instructional software and evaluates and dispenses materials for use at the elementary and secondary school levels.

Minnesota Educational Computing Consortium (MECC), is considered the largest educational network on the use of computers. Located in St. Paul, MECC coordinates and supports Minnesota's educational computing endeavors and develops and sells courseware for Apple. MECC publishes a newsletter and booklets and sponsors workshops to help educators start computer literacy programs in their schools. John R. Yeager, principal of Liberty Bell Elementary School in the Southern Lehigh School District in Pennsylvania, attended a MECC workshop in January 1980. Armed with new ideas about how to establish a microcomputer-supported computer literacy curriculum, Yeager returned home and spearheaded such a program for third-, fourth-, and fifth-graders in his district. By the beginning of the 1980-81 school year, he had prepared computer literacy objectives for these three grades and disseminated them to all district teachers from kindergarten through fifth grade. First- and second-graders used the Radio Shack micros for mathematics drill exercises. He also instituted in-service computer training for teachers.

The Microcomputer Resource Center at Teachers College

Columbia University conducts flexible-length workshops for teachers and administrators at the College or at school sites. The primary focus of the Center is teacher training. Workshops and seminars concern how to evaluate and select microcomputer software for school subjects.

The Microcomputer Education Applications Network (M.E.A.N.), a division of Education Turnkey Systems, Inc., is a consulting and research firm. This group has developed and disseminated software at the state and local levels for both administrative and instructional applications. The latter, however, is restricted to instructional packages for handicapped students. M.E.A.N. also conducts workshops and publishes a newsletter, the *M.E.A.N. Brief.*

QUEUE is another organization that publishes an informative monthly newsletter titled *Microcomputers in Education.* It provides hardware and software reviews and also publishes catalogues of software for specific vendors, such as Commodore, Radio Shack, and Apple.

EXXON indirectly aids microcomputer instruction. This giant corporation funds selected research proposals. Grants are restricted, however, to institutions of higher education. Professors could use award money to develop innovative software packages for school students.

The Association for Educational Communications and Technology (A.E.C.T.) is a professional organization committed to improving the use of instructional technology in the public schools. In October 1981 the U.S. Department of Education awarded A.E.C.T. $855,000 for Project BEST (Basic Education Skills through Technology), which is devoted to strengthening the capacity of state departments of education to work with local education agencies in the application of microcomputers and other new electronic technologies. During the 21-month contract period from November 1981 to July 1983, 43 state sites will be involved in the exchange of information and current learning experiences about the use of the new information technologies. This project, under the direction of Henry Ingle, employs technology as a means for sharing information through satellite teleconferencing, an electronic mail system, and other telecommunications linkages, including a telephone hotline. Moreover, microcomputers are being used to access several different data bases, such as bibliographic citations; experts and resource persons; forthcoming conferences, workshops, and seminars; and technological problems for each month.

Finally, the federal government is supporting microcomputer education with funding. One example is the Dade County, Florida Schools, which were awarded $300,000 of federal Title 4-B monies to institute microcomputers in their schools. Dade County purchased 162 microcomputers for use in 38 of the system's 255 elementary, junior high, and senior high schools. The new equipment, which included Atari 800 computers, disk drives, tape recorders for sound, and General Electric color television monitors, arrived in time for the 1981-82 school year. Title 4-B funding has now been merged with other programs under Chapter II of the Education Consolidation and Improvement Act of 1981. State departments of education are charged with allocating these funds.

A Glimpse of the Future

We are already living in the computer age. The advances in technology in the past 30 years have affected every aspect of our lives. What of the future?

Microcomputers will become faster and more versatile. A 32-bit microprocessor has already been invented by Intel. This wave-of-the-future microprocessor can access 16M bytes of main memory and up to one trillion bytes of storage, including secondary memory. Its execution speed is fantastic—a maximum two million instructions per second can be processed. Perhaps before the end of this century microcomputer capabilities will be equal to present-day large computers.

Microcomputers are destined to become smaller. Currently computer scientists and electronic engineers are working on developing a chip, about one micrometer square, that could hold a million transistors. If such devices were to be fabricated for microprocessors and memories, a microcomputer might be just slightly larger than a wristwatch. Seiko has just developed a television wristwatch that features a tiny screen; however the user must wear earphones for the audio component. Given this kind of device, fitted with the very tiny microprocessor, plus a miniature keyboard similar to those on Casio calculator wristwatches, a microcomputer wristwatch is a distinct possibility. If that Intel 32-bit microprocessor could be placed in that wristwatch, what a combination!

IBM is already working on a typewriter that takes voice dictation, displays the input on a screen for editing, and even types a hard copy. Adapting this kind of technology to the microcomputer would

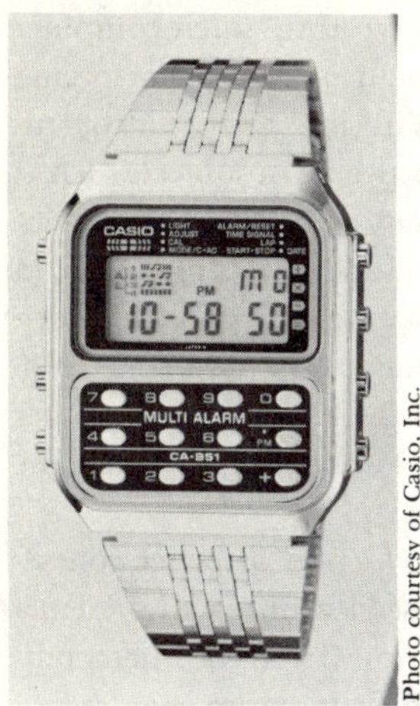

Photo courtesy of Casio, Inc.

This 20th century digital watch, properly modified, could become a 21st century tiny two-way talking computer.

definitely affect size. Clearly, a voice recognition input system, in place of a keyboard, however small, would reduce the size of a microcomputer. If a speech synthesizer output system, similar to that employed by Texas Instruments in their "talking" microprocessor toys, were coupled with the voice recognition system, a microcomputer so designed would both "hear" and "talk." The computer would have to recognize, interpret, and process natural language. Developing the technology for such capabilities is some distance in the future, but a tiny two-way talking wristwatch computer seems destined for sometime in the 21st century.

A new technique known as "interactive video" involves videodisk technology, another microprocessor-related medium. It has been used in conjunction with a touch-sensitive screen. A viewer touches a place on the screen and is given more detailed pictures about that place. For example, a trip through an art museum could be arranged if the viewer touches a picture of an art museum set in the context of a scene with other buildings in a city. M.I.T. has already effected this kind of technology. A company known as Discovision Associates is working with Apple Inc. to deliver this kind of exciting new medium. (See Barbara G. Gibson's article listed in the references.)

Another exciting development is the hologram. Laser technology can change the flat two-dimensional world of the screen to a realistic three-dimensional world via holography. Laser beams, characterized by straight, perfectly aligned light waves, are utilized in the science of holography to produce holograms, which are light images in three dimensions. (See the article by Jeff Hecht and Dick Teresi listed in the references.)

Implications for education based on the technological possibilities described above are numerous. Students wearing microcomputer wristwatches to school would have instantaneous problem-solving capabilities at their fingertips or voices. With interactive video, students could be taken from the general to the specific in subjects such as mathematics, natural sciences, and social sciences. Holograms in place of flat images in video computer games would add a new dimension, in more than one way, to the already fascinating avocation of video computer games. Game playing could become so popular that by 1990 college students will take courses given by a Department of Computer Games and Video Education. (See Bernie DeKoven's article listed in the references.)

There is already movement toward production of better courseware. Better courseware means computer-based learning will present a greater challenge to traditional learning styles. Given the microcomputer's strengths—color graphics, sound, entertainment, record management, and personal user control—by the 1990s computer-assisted learning will begin to compete seriously with books. By the onset of the 21st century, secondary storage media, such as diskettes and bubble-memory devices, could replace most books. David Moursund's futuristic chapter in *Introduction to Computers in Education for Elementary and Middle School Teachers*, contains many interesting thoughts on this topic.

As computers become more "user friendly" through better courseware and easier programming languages, computer literacy courses in elementary and secondary schools will spread and improve. Higher education computer literacy courses will have to keep pace. Arthur Luehrmann, in the March 1982 issue of *The Computing Teacher*, states there will be a need for three kinds of postsecondary computer literacy courses: 1) bonehead computing for students coming from schools where no computer literacy had been given; 2) orthodonture computing for students improperly trained at the lower levels; and 3) honors computer science for students with solid computer preparation.

For educators, a present and future concern is how best to prepare students for the microelectronics world in which they live. The ready availability of microcomputers and computer-based learning materials in both schools and homes means that parents and educators could form productive partnerships to bring technological instruction to students everywhere. Educators must look to technological advancements to make administration and teaching easier. They must consider microcomputers as tools that will release teachers to work individually with students. There will always be the need for interpersonal relationships between teachers and students. Computers cannot, nor ever will be able to, provide these services.

Appendix

Organizations Supporting Mirocomputer Education

Association for Educational Communications and Technology (A.E.C.T.)
1126 16th Street N.W.
Washington, D.C. 20036
(202) 466-4780
(services members only)

Apple Computer, Inc.
Foundation for the Advancement
of Computer Aided Education
20525 Mariani Avenue
Cupertino, CA 95014
(408) 973-2105

Association for Computing Machinery (A.C.M.)
11 West 42nd Street
New York, NY 10036
(212) 869-7440

Atari Institute
1196 Borregas Avenue
Sunnyvale, CA 94086
(408) 745-2666

Commodore Business Machines
487 Devon Park Drive
Wayne, PA 19087
(215) 687-9750

CONDUIT
P.O. Box 388
Iowa City, IA 52244
(319) 353-5789

EPIE Institute
Box 620
Stony Brook, NY 11790
(516) 246-8664

EXXON Education Foundation
111 West 49th Street
New York, NY 10020
(212) 398-2273

Microcomputer Education Applications Network (M.E.A.N.)
256 North Washington Street
Falls Church, VA 22046
(703) 536-2310

Microcomputer Resource Center
Teachers College Columbia University
525 West 121st Street
New York, NY 10027
(212) 678-3740

MicroSIFT
Northwest Regional Educational Laboratory (N.R.E.L.)
300 S.W. 6th Avenue
Portland, OR 97204
(503) 248-6800

Minnesota Educational Computing Consortium (M.E.C.C.)
2520 Broadway Drive
St. Paul, MN 55113
(612) 376-1101

QUEUE, Inc.
5 Chapel Hill Drive
Fairfield, CT 06432
(203) 372-6761

Radio Shack
A Division of Tandy Corporation
1300 One Tandy Center
Fort Worth, TX 76102
(817) 390-3011

References

Aycock, Ellen; Frankowski, Elaine N.; and Franta, W. R. *Microcomputers in Institutions of Higher Education: Their Past, Present and Future Characteristics and Uses.* Minneapolis, Minn.: University of Minnesota, 1981.

This is a well-researched reference book that includes both technical material about microcomputers and interest features such as their history and their penetration into higher education.

Baker, Justine. *Computers in the Curriculum*, Fastback No. 82. Bloomington, Ind.: Phi Delta Kappa Educational Foundation, 1976.

This booklet deals with the necessity of computer education for teachers. Two in-house surveys pertinent to the topic are included. The text has historical significance.

Bohl, Marilyn. *Information Processing,* 3rd ed. Chicago: Science Research Associates, 1980.

This is a computer awareness textbook suitable for undergraduate college students and general readership.

Capron, H. L., and Williams, Brian K. *Computers and Data Processing.* Menlo Park, Calif.: The Benjamin/Cummings Publishing Company, 1982.

This is a computer awareness textbook suitable for undergraduate college students and general readership.

Cornish, Blake M. "The Smart Machines of Tomorrow: Implications for Society." *The Futurist,* August 1981, pp. 5-13.

DeKoven, Bernie. "Computer Games: The Future Present." *Personal Computing,* June 1982, pp. 68-70, 72, 122-123.

EPIE Materials Report 98/99m Microcomputer Courseware/Microprocessor Games. Stony Brook, N.Y.: EPIE Institute, 1981.

Evans, Christopher. *The Micro Millennium.* New York: Viking Press, 1980. This text addresses the microelectronics revolution and what the future might be like in light of this revolution.

Freiberger, Stephen, and Chew, Paul Jr. *A Consumer's Guide to Personal Computing and Microcomputers,* 2nd ed. Rochelle Park, N.J.: Hayden Book Company, Inc., 1980.

This is an excellent book for getting acquainted with microcomputers. Technical material is relatively easy to follow.

Gibson, Barbara G. "The Electronic Canvas." *Apple,* November 1981, pp. 2-4.

Golden, Frederic. "Here Come the Microkids." *Time,* 3 May 1982, pp. 50-56.

Goor, Jeanette; Melmed, Arthur; and Farris, Elizabeth. *Student Use of Computers in Schools, Fall 1980.* FRSS Report No. 12. Washington, D.C.: National Center for Education Statistics, 1982.

Hecht, Jeff, and Teresi, Dick. "Sun Guns." *Omni,* May 1982, pp. 61-62, 64, 94-95.

Identifying and Getting Your Share of the School Market for Microcomputers. Westport, Conn.: Market Data Retrieval, October 1981.

Luehrmann, Arthur. "Computer Literacy." *The Computing Teacher,* March 1982, pp. 24-26. [Reprinted by permission from the EDUCOM Bulletin (Winter 1981): 14-15, 24.]

Lule, Jack. "Video Jocks Versus the Quarter-Eaters." *Today, The Inquirer Magazine,* 24 January 1982, pp. 18-21, 25-27.

    This is the Sunday supplement to *The Philadelphia Inquirer.*

Malone, Thomas W. *What Makes Things Fun to Learn? A Study of Intrinsically Motivating Computer Games.* Palo Alto, Calif.: XEROX Palo Alto Research Center, 1980.

    This interesting publication can be obtained from XEROX PARC Cognitive and Instructional Sciences Group, 3333 Coyote Hill Road, Palo Alto, CA 94304.

McGee, Mark G. "Human Spatial Abilities: Psychometric Studies and Environmental, Genetic, Hormonal, and Neurological Influences." *Psychological Bulletin* 86 (September 1979): 889-918.

Moursund, David. *Introduction to Computers in Education for Elementary and Middle School Teachers.* Eugene, Ore.: International Council for Computers in Education, 1981.

    This is a self-instruction book about how to use computers for instruction. The eighth and final chapter concerning future possibilities is especially interesting. The essence of that chapter can be found on pages 17-23 of the November 1981 issue of *The Computing Teacher.*

__________ "Microcomputers Will Not Solve the Computers-In-Education Problem." *AEDS* (Association for Educational Data Systems) *Journal* (Fall 1979): 31-39.

__________ *Precollege Computer Literacy: A Personal Approach.* Eugene, Ore.: International Council for Computers in Education, Department of Computer and Information Science, University of Oregon, 1981.

    This booklet opens with three short historical perspectives of computers. The first is from a technical viewpoint; the second, educational; the third, computer literacy. Then a detailed exposition of computer literacy is presented in light of its five categories. A glossary is included.

Norman, Colin. "The New Industrial Revolution: How Microelectronics May Change the Workplace," *The Futurist,* February 1981, pp. 30-40.

O'Brien, James A. *Computers in Business Management,* 3d ed. Homewood, Ill.: Richard D. Irwin, 1982.

    This text is intended for undergraduate business majors but is also suited for general readership since it is a computer awareness text.

Papert, Seymour. *Mindstorms: Children, Computers, and Powerful Ideas.* New York: Basic Books, 1980.

This little book presents Papert's thinking about learning and LOGO, the computer language for young children.

Poirot, J.; Taylor, R.; and Powell, J. "Teacher Education." *Topics: Computer Education for Elementary and Secondary Schools.* New York: Association for Computing Machinery, 1981.

Rogers, J. B., and Austing, D. "Computer Science in Secondary Schools: Recommendations for a One-Year Course." *Topics: Computer Education for Elementary and Secondary Schools.* New York: Association for Computing Machinery, 1981.

Spencer, Donald D. *Data Processing: An Introduction with BASIC,* 2d *ed.* Columbus, Ohio: Charles E. Merrill Publishing Co., 1982.

This is a computer awareness text suitable for undergraduate college students and general readership.

Taylor, Robert P., ed. *The Computer in the School: Tutor, Tool, Tutee.* New York: Teachers College Press, 1980.

This text features a collection of articles written by five distinguished professors in the computer education field. Although not exclusively written about microcomputers, ideas expressed could apply to microcomputers.

Thé, Lee. "Educational Software for the Home." *Personal Computing.* June 1982, pp. 48-52, 102-103, 106, 108, 110, 114.

Uston, Ken. *Mastering PAC-MAN.* New York: A Signet Book, New American Library, 1981.

This is an entertaining book suitable for all video arcade game buffs or those desiring high PAC-MAN scores.

Watson, Nancy, R., ed. *Microcomputers in Education: Getting Started, Conference Proceedings.* Tempe, Ariz.: Arizona State University, 1981.

This volume contains a collection of papers presented on 16-17 January 1981 at Arizona State University. Topics cover computer literacy, microcomputer management systems, network systems for schools, teacher training, programming, and computer-assisted instruction. There is also a special General Information Section concerning BASIC computer books, computer journals, computer-related films, microcomputer manufacturers, and software vendors.

———— *Microcomputers in Education: Uses for the '80s, Conference Proceedings.* Tempe, Ariz.: Arizona State University, 1982.

This volume contains a collection of papers presented on 15-16 January 1982 at Arizona State University. Topics cover impact of new federalism on microcomputers, microcomputer courseware, microcomputers in instructional research, microcomputer uses in schools, placement of microcomputers in schools, research and projects, administrative uses, computer-assisted instruction, literacy, and programming. A glossary and journals section is included.

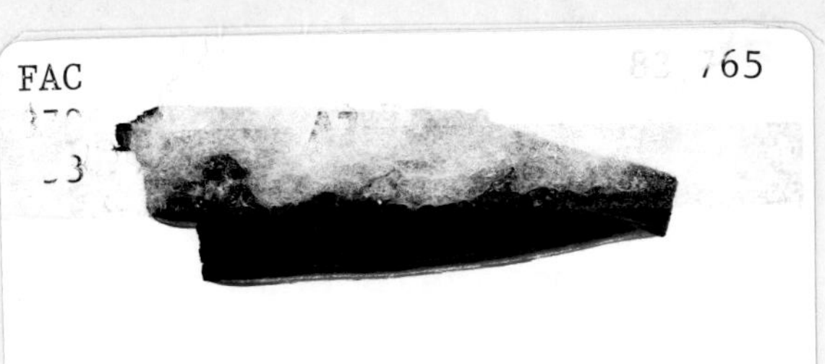

DEC 22 '66			